Hard Bargain
Poems

Heather Treseler

LILY POETRY REVIEW BOOKS

Copyright © 2025 by Heather Treseler
Published by Lily Poetry Review Books
223 Winter Street
Whitman, MA 02382

https://lilypoetryreview.blog/

ISBN: 978-1-957755-54-0

Cover painting: Vincent van Gogh, *The Novel Reader (Liseuse de romans)*, 1888

For Marita and Fred Treseler

"What would happen if one woman told the truth about her life? The world would split open."

—Muriel Rukeyser, from "Käthe Kollwitz"

Table of Contents

Bantry, 1910

Cool muddied March: chill pierces her sweater unless she keeps
  a move on, gets home before dark. When she sizes the bull up

from behind, what is the smell like—sharp tang of male and manure,
  rye grass and sudor? His testicles, lonely clapper of a bell, a rump

five or six times the size of her skull. At home, an hour of chores
  on either side of supper, and that supper shared: eating while

spooning her baby brother's softened porridge. Then mucking
  the mares' stalls. A girl's life the tending of orifices not her own.

But she can save a half hour if she cuts across the field. Old bull,
  sun-drunk, dozes, jowls dripping, and she feels her limbs fill

with brisk resolve like a bucket plunged into icy well, and she takes
  off, brogans squelching in graveled muck that midway sucks off

a shoe: she stops to pluck it, strange leather flower, sound rousing
  the bull to his intruder—so she runs fierce now, arms splayed,

earth rumbling under beast brunt, and in five strides, she reaches
  the fence and somersaults, headlong, thwacking her thin back

against the stone post as she feels the tug and long rip of what
  he caught: white flag on the point of his horn: half her skirt.

Not the last time she makes it in a stitch—across the Atlantic,
  rail tracks, Scollay skids, dance hall alley, steep snowy hill

to the Brighton hospital—becoming my spry named forebear,
  not another obedient girl, maimed and trapped Europa.

                —i.m. Margaret Spillane (1894-1989)

Leda

She had put on his knowledge. But he did not know
she also took her share of power—the Yeats scholar,
swanning into department meetings with his china
teacup and armorial tweed. She had first met him
at the new faculty luncheon where he waxed wise
about local real estate and research funds. Later,
she wondered: when had he planned to tell her he
chaired the tenure committee? Before the first drink?
After he stepped, uninvited, into a kiss inside her door?
He styled himself a man of Ted Hughes intensities—
his ghosts, his crows, his horsey eyes that brimmed
with mention of Tennyson. Woundedness, his game
with women, like Zeus donning feather boas—
that preposterous bird suit. She knew the trade:

her acquiescence, his backing. Given the stakes, should
she take the sacking? If she declined and he retaliated,
she'd have the long fraught duty of making her case—
the grim air of jurisprudence in the HR office, some
dim thirty-year-old official unable to spell 'fellatio.'
But if she accepted one night's trespass, she could cite
the landlord's scruples and get him out before breakfast.
Clearly, he did not see she was from Sparta: a generation
of women who, as girls, watched mothers suffer—
and swore they would never pay that tax without
burning down every last priapic Troy. So when he
finished with a birdie flourish, she pet the little beak
and dry webbed feet imagining how, some years from
now, a bright axe would fall and she would baste him.

Birth of Venus

Botticelli, and the old dream of a child
    born without pain, her beauty
        sired cleanly by the sea

and the cast-off genital blood of a god.
    Art departs from a strict
        monastic tradition

of holy books and stained glass used
    to school the illiterate in their
        sinfulness, their lives'

endless task of contrition. But you can
    only get so far on pedantry,
        sublimation. Bodies

want something akin to their own flesh,
    desiring. And who is to say
        the genial portly son

of a tanner could not also save the soul
    at the Quattrocento, having been
        tutored for centuries

in fear, abnegation: chided by clerics guilty
    of wildest gluttony and lust,
        venery of the young

and vulnerable? (The artist met a cardinal
    in Verona known to relish
        the hymens of nuns,

orphans as young as eight.) So the artist,
   doubling as Cronus with his brush,
      castrates the wayward

fathers, hurls foaming parts into a sea
   of tempera, applied to canvas,
      and centuries' violation

birth a pagan goddess, held aloft, scallop
   shell gleaming like a vulva given
      back to its own pleasure.

Blue Madonna

Mother, less a noun than predicate
in the daily liturgy of care for a second
body, childhood's parade of sensation
as in tickle, here come the elephants,
the clown of a graham cracker bobbing
in its dunk tank of milk, a trapeze act
of noodles sidling down the tines.

A laughter not required to repress itself.
To Winnicott, a "good enough mother"
allowed the adult to survive customary
traumas, hostile environs: how the child
is first held forecasts her skill as friend
and lover, artist or beholder, suspended
freely in another's eyes or hands.

Mothering owing something, improbably,
to the brutal Medicis, murderers who
adored fine art and paid for the flecks
of gold and lapis lazuli in the luminous
blue madonnas, iconizing the tableau
of mother and child. As in this portrait
by Fra Lippi where the mother, arms

outstretched, fixes her gaze and speaks
her son's name as she greets the wobbly
haloed toddler god with almost the same
gesture with which she will receive
a flaccid corpse on the dark afternoon
he is finally let down from his last
willful climb of that thorned tree.

Barter

Her father was drying out again at some discreet
   rehab in bucolic lake-pocked New Hampshire:

a Christian outfit with gilded bibles, pastoral care,
   and the mountainous granite eye of God.

She dressed me up like a fruity bonbon, tasseled
   and pink bowed, and drove three hours north,

stopping to nurse and change the nappies. He'd
   been sober three weeks. In words I can neither

conjure nor recall, she set down terms: if he wanted
   to watch that baby girl grow he had to quit

the bottle. One slip, and the kiddo was gone.
   I did not learn of their arrangement until years

after he was dead. But I think of the hours cruised
   to Glenn Miller in his plush tricked-out Buick;

how he showed me off to cashiers, clerks, crossing
   guards; how, flying in his dentist's hydraulic

chair, I was the dauphin or destined for the moon;
   how gently he shined the tops of red patent shoes.

A child can be a gift, raised like a chalice, wielded
   like a crowbar. Whatever I had cost my mother

in the trouble of my birth, she took what her body
   made, proud pawn, and drove her hardest bargain.

Cinder

This is a story of fire, ash, and a girl
falling into a tall blaze that singed
her side. This is the girl, now thirty,
now a woman looking into a mirror
at a square of red that marks her back
like the mustard stripe of a garter snake
she saw, once, its jaws unlatched, eating

a whole frog. This her gratitude that it
lives, red story, under a blouse, under
covers, under the day's thin or bulky
sweater: there, without any telling,
a memento of fire, ash, the day she
fell into a blaze. Is this the shape,
she wonders, of memory's scar—

the changing or unchanging script
of sure hands that plucked her from
fire as fast as her side had tasted it?
This is he who brought her flame
to his chest and held her there, in its
long wailed extinguishing. This is
the hole burnt in a little gray jacket,

in a purple sweater, in a tiny undershirt:
burnt, its half-dollar of light, into skin,
its pale white unfinishing. This is the one
who attended, unflinching, with salve
and debriding, the dress and undressing
of a red wound for which he assigned
her no blame, making no wrong of her

unbridled dance in wooded dark on fall
slicked leaves by the campfire, its long
licks of flame, her trying to keep up
with older children, just the same.
This is their shared understanding
of the pleasure of fire, the wonder
of heat warming the face. This is

the grown woman, tracing the ledger
of care, recalling the tree-like smell
of eucalyptus, gauzy wrappings,
the ritual pain in dressing, undressing.
This is her wondering why she did not
then learn the cost of fearlessness,
the danger in courting fire, ash-making

flame. This is the woman at night,
slipped from bed, standing in a moon's
quarter arc of light beside a silver
glinting mirror, nightgown hoisted
shyly to shoulder as she reads, again,
the shape and cinder of the story.
And there is her lover, fast asleep

in his separate dreams, hours after
holding his tender mouth to her
chest, salving her there. This is she
who scours the inked dark after
love's sweet unsettling, looking
for a mark of girlhood's dance, what
blaze and fiery ash brought her here.

Tenancy

I am duchess of it, this rented apartment,
each misshelved book and errant plant—
each ship deck slanted floor and leaky
faucet, these fourteen balky windows
(from some unlicensed postwar cousin
back in the day), light switches wired
all the wrong way—like fetishists, turned
on when they're meant to be turned off.

But it is my unmade bed and 1982 stove.
And from my desk I hear the city hum
with dog diplomats, throatily negotiating
biscuits or treaties, rush hour horns' blazing
impatience, a leaf blower's attempt at anger
management. I can see the Silvios' robin egg
grotto for Mary; Gerard's plump terracotta
Buddha; and the Smiths' inflatable snowman

daily losing his stature this warm December,
assuming child's pose by noon—as if to prostrate
himself to the seasonal demand for bustle,
ribboned bundles, and nutmegged cheer.
And I am here, on a second floor, where I can
strut naked behind a shut door, close the blinds
and drink my own nine-dollar wine
in eight hundred square feet I lock and call

mine: petite redoubt, drafty bunker, green
zone of quiet. Early mornings, I sit in one
of two large chairs with my dog-eared books
and itinerant ghosts—generations who shadow
my page, those who hardly knew an afternoon's
rest, a week to read, loaf, or be (for themselves)
undressed. These spare unshared rooms, these
unpledged hours an estate, an inheritance.

Letters of Ida Bauer to Her Mother

Vienna, c. 1900

I.

Dr. Freud of the neat gray beard and muffled
sighs, the dark pressed suits and ascot ties:
he promises, mother, that the sharp pains
of all last summer—what cuts across my face
like sharded glass—will subside, and with them
my cough, if I talk freely of the fears that
crowd in, upon me, in the narrow dark.

If I bring myself into the lamplight or stippled
sun, filtered through the damask curtains beside
his couch, if I examine what it is I have hidden
from myself like auntie's dog, which feigns
forgetting until even he cannot remember
where it was he put her fan or silk slipper,
what it was he stole and made an hour's toy.

II.

Today, mother, I told Freud about Herr K
cornering me in the garden behind the old
woodshed. Insinuations at tea: all his fuss
about spoons and cream, the cup he insisted
stirring for me. Then his leg, pressed
against mine, throughout dinner. Herr K,
married, jowled, nearly as old as father!

Yet the doctor seemed to think none of it
mattered. *Wasn't it*, he asked, *flattering
to have attention from such an accomplished
gentleman? To be admired, found pretty
and worthy? To be sought so gently?
Didn't Herr K*, he asked, *make me
feel happy and womanly? Lucky?*

III.

But is it luck, mother, or the typical rub of fate? Each
girl, reborn a crisis when she is no longer thought
a child, deserving protection, but a young woman,
ripe and blushing, ready (it is supposed) to be
taken from her innocence, made to travel
the fabled journey from fruit to fruition,
courtship to love and children, and the repose

worn by matrons as honor—or mask of exhaustion,
an eerie stillness akin to death. Isn't the story often
disaster? Hasty feeling, crescendos of innuendo,
coyness, then castigation? Can a woman ever
say plainly what she wants? I have no interest
in Herr K or old men sagging in their bones
like smug children loitering in unkempt beds.

IV.

Dreams, Freud says, are the soul's dialect
of desire. In analysis, I hear its whispering,
its intimations a secret language of my being.
How strange—or sensible—a dialogue between
the head and body. How bizarre that the mind
can regard each limb, each run of skin, each
finger as integral or as a perfect stranger.

The body, he claims, is already in communion,
but the mind is a minotaur of ideal and desire:
it thinks, we yearn; it obeys, and we ache
with hunger. To leave off my woolen terror
and cure my pain, to find a love worthy
of its name, perhaps I have only to listen
to my flesh speak, nakedly, to my soul.

Berggasse 19

Much can be accomplished in the pregnant
pause, in the gap between wish and warrant:
at such intervals, I studied her brunette crown

and the pale travel of skin along her hair's part—
uneven as a homemade envelope, and the little
black boots beneath her cloaked ankles, resting

on the far side of the davenport: small mute feet,
clutched like darkly burrowed animals, asleep
in winter's decay of leaves. Because I knew

Ida's father, because I myself have played
in the masque of public life, a learned man
attending the ill and addled, because I too

have suffered the schism between desire and others'
appraisal, because I have worked the wormwood
of id into smoothed superego, and because publicity

whets in men a need for privacy, interior, and
the solace of womanly affection: I endeavored
to cure her, to restore trusting girlish instincts

(as in the tropism of Alpine ferns): what leads them
to seek the warmth of manly esteem. Little black
boots at the far edge of the davenport; her delicate

crown as soft and brown as a rabbit's skull; symptoms
of *petite hystérie* coinciding with advances from Herr K
and the onset of her menses, mistaken for a deadly

wound. She dreams of house fires, her long hair
aflame; the jewelry box of her genitals barely
rescued from conflagration. At the end, Otto,

of each hour, there is a deep threshing ache
in my temples. And elsewhere. As we have
noted, transference can border on contagion.

Vigilance must be maintained. Those dainty
boots, brunette crown, her thin-hipped tensile
body resting beneath the wainscoting lined

with my carved imagoes—Venus of Krems,
Venus of Willendorf—goddesses of fertility,
their lived pleasure evident in dimpled flesh.

In Ida, I can discern the lure of exogamy: sexual
union with another clan's prized women, allure
of the foreign gradually made intimate, familiar.

Eros alive in that gap, in the long pregnant pause
between wish and warrant, in a young virgin's
dreams and fears, and how I yearn to answer.

Callas, 1954

Back in Athens with your mother, you took bread and wine
on a Eucharistic spoon from long-bearded priests: religion

makes formal the desire for transformation.

A yearning to purify, escape the body. Or New York City,
where your mother realized she was no longer in love. You,

the subplot, daughter and sister of beautiful

women busy with heartbreak's intrigue. Finding your talent,
you honed its talons under a stairwell in the dark: religion

makes formal the desire for transformation.

Perfecting the instrument of voice, you became *prima donna
assoluta* of audiences in Venice and Verona, but demurred roles

you judged suited to a lithe girl, someone

appearing in a narrow bodice without shame. *Avoirdupois*,
the regality of your large pale body, flower of flesh,

what became enemy. One year, in seclusion,

you lost a hundred pounds, emerged as svelte as Hepburn.
'Opera is the battlefield,' you opined as you took audiences,

husband, lovers: art makes formal the desire

for transformation. Beauty a devouring god. Halved, you sang
bel canto until your voice winnowed, collapsed. After the final

tour, you took a house in Paris in which stairwell

echoes let you feel the famed vibrato—as an old colonel, asleep
by open window, runs through a grassy clearing in his dream.

Nervosa

You began eating again not on account
of the long nights of fevered half-sleep
or the fine hair mossing your arms

or the cold that shadowed you like
an ice moon of Pluto. You estranged
yourself from nature with calm

indifference, letting breasts retreat
to apostrophes on torso's sentence
that summer of undesire. Away

from home's old moorings, you
felt like a suitcase gone rogue—
sprung loose on a hot tarmac

or frenzied freeway, girlhood's
embarrassments flapping freely
in the wind. Noontimes, you sat

at the Fill-a-Buster Café, drunk
on the smell of melting sandwiches,
numb to winks and nods, on break

from a summer job filing bills
honed into law, cool type of
governances. But on that day

you could not remember what
you had read in the newspaper,
natural disasters muddled with

wars, celluloid scenes of ruin.
Words swam unfixed from
meaning, and you knew then

what would happen if you did
not pay rent on your tenanted
body, if you did not go blinking

into the day's wincing brightness,
leaving off glassed interiors
and closets of compliance

for the muddy errands of hunger,
the aching notes of a singer,
flesh flowered on her bones.

Daphne on Being Wood

I never meant it to be permanent: this body house
   of wood, this foliating iron lung, these brachia

of branched leaves that were my exeunt and leave-taking.
   I did not intend to remain a tree forever—perhaps

for a few years of Apollo's high-octane testosterone,
   the nymph mania that sparks in men between

a spendthrift prime and mid-aged fear of death. Cycles
   of tumescence spin longer among the gods—

and there is no one rutting season, so a girl must spot
   the symptoms: late-night fistfights; musky smells;

predawn prowls of car parks, beaches; beer cans strewn
   in the strangest of places. Apollo was the worst.

He stank of horse dung and char and stood squinting
   at the sky, wizened like a bathhouse lecher worn

by years of salt and sun, orgies of ale and tail. Too old
   to be a beach boy but inflamed by a gold-tipped

arrow wedged slightly south of his cock, he chased me
   like a thing possessed, gripped by divine selfishness.

He did not know Peneus, my father, had taught me to run,
   honing my flight instinct to win the local footrace

by twenty yards. What I didn't know was that I couldn't
   outrace a god. When I felt Apollo's breath scorch

the valley of my neck with his back-alley intention, when
   he sped in reach of my disheveling hair, hunting me

to some duck blind or grove of desolation, I saw the scene
   he intended. I saw a gibbous moon's gleam in his teeth.

I screamed out prayers, pleas, imprecations, and suddenly
   a change was wrought in me—I felt my womb fall

to my feet and score its roots in earth; my legs filled to one
   solid girth, grooving to bark; and my arms sprung open

like spontaneous umbrellas. I writhed like Sibyl nearing
   prophecy, but my wail was walled into a muteness

beyond wonder: no longer had I mouth or face. My features
   receded into whorls of wood, an astigmatic grain, these

rings of surprise that wrung through what had been my body,
   piercingly hot then chill, my blood changing to a pulpy

sap burbling in my veins. I peered up at my rooftop of leaves—
   had I become an oak, sycamore, or elm? I did not learn

what I was until spring, when they called me laurel, and spoke
   in hushed suspicious tones of the tragedies of naivete

and girlish stubbornness as if escape ever required less than
   total transformation. As if, born woman, I had not been

made to suffer ritual perils, or the hydraulic power of beauty
   and its maturation, fevered desire in others and in myself,

my reluctant coda of resistance. Mortals often wish to unwound
   themselves of time, forgetting that clocks bring anguish

to some end. The morning after I evaded my captor, I stretched
   my new several feet into cooling loam, girlhood's promissory

body changed to a joke on permanence: a woman in her prime,
   immured in the living mausoleum of a tree. Denied choice,

I found my volition. My limbs now crown runners, rhetoricians,
   those who track hard truth over distance, distressing the old

romance that all are given to themselves, foremost and free—
   and honoring those who remember a girl named Daphne.

Persephone's Postcard

The dead, they are always descending
   like mustachioed men in Magritte's
painting, so many bowler hats sailing
   through a pale blue Belgian sky.

Heavy souls—freighted with evil,
   leaden sorrow, or the insomniac
stare of bald regret—crash all night
   against the stone gates of Hades

and stumble, wrecked, along the neon
   strip mall on the far side of Styx,
a tinsel town where hawkers sell
   the newbies musky perfumes,

condensed from their memories,
   and half-hour holograms of any
one beloved thing: pets or dill pickles,
   a niece or ball glove, something

to cop one last recessional feel. All
   night, unhappy shades rain on
the earthen roof of the root cellar
   boudoir I share with my husband

who promised, after snatching me
   from behind, from the white flowers
of Nysa, that I'd grow used to traffic
   of the dead, the continual thump

of souls in the night, above my head,
   like the asphalt slap of a slowly
deflating basketball. He promised,
   wielding his bird-tipped scepter,

to make in me another music in which
　　I'd hear myself without my jealous
mother's cautionary antiphon. In truth,
　　though Hades stole me to his lair,

he gave me to my pleasure, enticing me
　　to be greedy, to take and take his potent
seed into my store until I glowed dark
　　with satisfactions. His lust and coy

protest at my departures came to mark
　　time, to cadence more than our seasonal
passions. Between the knock of souls
　　above and our tender mock-Bartók below,

small sprays of earth fell almost nightly
　　from our ceiling. Most mornings, I wake
to the taste of summered grass, soil raked
　　through my hair, a snail burrowing

his glistening trail into loamy blankets
　　where Hades turns, each winter night,
for the press of my lips and obliging limbs
　　to receive him, his almost mythic want:

thanatos seeking *eros* to spring him to life
　　again, granting some vital answer
to death's absolute value of Zed.
　　Once Demeter's obedient daughter,

cosseted to her buxom pride, now wife
　　to a god of night who bears it all
away: I tell you, friend, in our green
　　unruly nocturnes, often mistaken

for raw shades' rueful laughter, there is
   a reminder: Hades may husband
a fertile knowing beauty, but I
   remain death's regnant queen.

Demeter: Calendar Girl

You can't imagine what Persephone hauls
home in her hair, what lives in those marshy
dreadlocks: Stygian snails, fat pill bugs, bits

of shag carpet, mud-matted tails of water
rats. Each equinox, my daughter clambers
above ground, trailing detritus like a bridal

train, and I give her an hour-long shampoo.
Mortals call it a "power wash"—as if potency
entailed absolution. I assume a tripod stance,

like a firefighter, and amp up that nozzle's
stream, ridding Sephone of the spores
and species, the loam and languor of her

other home, that dank cavern beside oblivion
where she pays a penance for having been
born beautiful. My daughter, the wife of death.

In truth, abduction is a mother's second worst
nightmare after blistering fevers, anaphylaxis,
furtive pneumonia, toxic shock, or immolation

via bongs, boys, car wrecks, Roman candles.
(Hence the need for car seats, fire sprinklers,
seatbelts, sunscreen, inflammable pajamas.)

Like all mothers, I thought I'd kept her safe.
But ten years ago, Hades envied his brother
Zeus for his glammed up wife and sidelong

sport with nymphs and goatherds. Ten years
ago, I let Sephone play in flower-pleated fields,
not knowing my brother hid nearby, watching

her race through meadows, and frolic in bright
sun, unaware of danger lurking there. He seized
her by the belt and hair, muffling her panicked

cries as he slid her underground, turning harvest
into darkest theft in violation of every rule—
ancient, exogamous, statutory—taking from

her what should only be freely given,
taking from me the yield of my life.
Unspeakable, a sin against all law.

Whoever thought sibling rivalry could
turn to such catastrophe? When Hades
snatched my daughter, hoarding her

laughter, he robbed the woods of wind,
fields of rain, and galaxies of stars that
bud, in summer, from her fair shoulders.

Bereft, crazed, not knowing where she had
gone or how to find her, I wandered miles,
straight through the leather of my shoes—

a pilgrim beyond prayer, beyond the gods
and groveling. I bared my chest to sun
and sirocco, issuing a wail that echoed over

land, stunting crops in their greening sleeves,
curdling milk in the gentlest cows, scaring
bees back inside their famished hives.

A long winter came, refused to leave. Ache
gnawed at the thinned branches of trees,
ravaged as burned-out fuselage after sudden

war. Gone was the deep saddling joy that
had once hummed in me, the sweet fever
in which I took Zeus to the loom of my wish

for child. Before she had a name, I had dreamt
the lineaments and light of my daughter's face.
I had heard the echo of her toddling feet, seen

the trusting fondness in her gaze, known
a tenderness ignorant of malice. All that
Hades trespassed in his lustful clamor.

When I learned who had stolen her,
I fought to stay my hand, wanting
death's surrender, a quick descent

to the birdless place to find where
he had her caged. Months, I did
not sleep, hollowed to the horror

of my daughter serving the nightly
pleasure of the dead land's king.
How could a clod of bristle beard

and foul hands husband any woman?
Dire, the situation. Direct, my intervention.
Though here most stories have it wrong.

It was *I* who sewed pomegranate seeds
into the hems of all her skirts: mothering
is imagining a narrative beyond the first

emergency: tourniquets doubling as parachutes,
prophylactics hidden in passport jackets.
Because she had eaten the red seeds of earth,

pods of memory, fertility, blood, and birth,
I could plead to Zeus for her just return.
Each spring, my daughter is mine again.

Though a dozen goddesses squawk
and squaw over the throne of heaven,
only one is unrivaled queen of hell.

If I must share her with Plouton, I'll cherish
each ascent and yearly flower, each nestled
night and summered hour. Perhaps we love

the best those who must recede from us
before they can return; on them, we
lavish. For them, we ache and yearn.

Aubade

Jackhammers jolt me awake: the hard hats are back
   with handheld thunder, sheathed skulls crest
the gray asphalt, fractured neatly as a split sternum.
   Upstairs, I watch the scrum of tanned faces, Mars

helmets the unnatural bright shades of candy as they work
   the street's cavity, digging sandy strata to a matrix
of pipes, cables, and wires: a city's hidden anatomy, its
   fascia, viscera, bowels, and liver, what lives flexing

and flushing in hundreds of conveyances below roadways,
   trim berm, modest trees, and prim hedges that nod
at a vestige of Arcadian hunger. Yet the broken road isn't
   a trench lined with the bones of comrades, heroes

from the last resistance. It is a grave-sized pocket of dirt
   in which some toil, so that our surfaces stay seemly.
From above, still in the bed fog before embodied thought,
   I watch an officer direct a thread of passing traffic

as a tabby cat circles, in wide berth, this raw new mouth
   of earth, this spiraling staircase to Hades: it scans for
a thin tail or scurry, as some unlucky mortal (or morsel)
   awakes and unburies, fresh to the world's appetites.

Quarantine

Because I have not forgotten
the ceremony of our nakedness,

my hunger that begs the question—

because I woke in the early dark
thinking I was again a child, duplex

wall echoing the neighbor's snore

as some reprise of *parents, parents*
heavy in their slumber, sighing out

of sync with each other in an old

wooden house of draft and splinter
where we kept warm and eyed one

another in the theater called family

where the acts were made to seem
spontaneous, lines unrehearsed,

a plot cast by some fate or garage god,

some latter-day method director who
tied us like monkeys to a kitchen table

or made the eldest drag, for days, a pot

of ugly soup, a broken chair. I woke then,
fully—and was forty. Not a child packed

in a tight cigarette box of fiery white

carcinogens. I wanted to call, to hear
the dark carnal startle in your voice,

to conjure your unstudied touch all

along my limbs in a warm bed meadow
not a hundred-odd miles and plague away.

Halfway

Midlife, midsummer, and an infatuation
with the idea of leisure as I watch
the paper-white moths fan against the dark
door's louvered glass and trees rustle in preamble
to an afternoon storm's erotic tempest.
There is pleasure in the slack grins
of playground swings, a neighbor's dog
warming his mottled belly on sunned brick,
clouds that burl as if with mammalian feeling
as they caravan across the sky. Had my loneness
outlived its purpose? An illness appeared
as if in answer. Vertigo, fever, fog in thought.
Terror in the long staircase between words,
syntax no banister. Years before, lost
at King's Cross, tugging my suitcase like a stubborn
pet, summer dress wrinkled, dishabille—
everyone had hurtled on past as I stood
under the giant clock, its gilt gaze the pupil
of an aging empire or an infant god.
Now I was moored in bed, wondering
what kind of animal was my body, its purpose
and ease dispatched to districts unknown,
its wakeful hours a dialogue with pain.
Asleep, I often dreamt of sleep, an orange
cat named Marmalade, banter at the tables
of friends. I dreamt I wrote a letter
to the child I once had been, and to the older
woman I might still become—with assurance
that I no longer owed a debt to anyone, no debt
to joy—whether it appeared as unexpected
as the woods' lady slipper, its flag of fuchsia
spread over molding winter leaves,
or as two silhouettes in a shared
window where the days might undress

and redress, folding quietly, one upon the other.
Death itself might be akin to conversation
with that one lover or the closest of friends:
event, held aloft, turned subject to thought,
examination. In midlife, a harvest moon drew
taut the string between sea and horizon,
and I began to learn what kind was my animal,
wherefore the latecomers' train—
what specie of choice might remain
along my hands' meridian line.

Sapphic

All night, the heat pipes clanked
and chortled, whined and groaned
like two cantankerous old lovers
practiced in the habit of each other's
pleasure. All night, I wandered lonely
as the sheep of unsleep, badger
of worry, skunk of longing,
all hungry nose and restless tail.

Shadows clung to the furred dark
scarved around my shoulders,
tucked behind my narrow knees:
all of me postured around your
absence like the archaic statue
tilled from a Tuscan hillside
by a farmer's plow that clocked
its dirt-rouged marble brow.

From manure and loam to fine
museums on loan: even icons
must make a little money, earn
their keep in our esteem. I study
a trio of *Orantes* from an ancient
tomb: three women with their
arms outstretched around a lost
object, negative space giving

their tilted hips, listing breasts,
and nearsighted looks definition.
No wonder, last night, I couldn't
find my glasses. Better to gaze
at corroded figures than study
the unremarkable ruin of one's
body, etched with orbits around
the sun, an almost uniform no one.

So lack gives to the lyre, draws
longing into language. I sit,
mulling phrases, like a young
child learning syllables' lock-and-
key specificity, earning the gentling
touch, warm scent, and familiar
voice of another—or the eye
of the night's moon mother.

Sparrow

Is the bird lured, as I am, by the sale on plush towels?
 A flattering version of itself in plated glass? Or is it

seduced by cold air as the mall door swings wide and it flies
 inside to bob, Pentecostal flame, over heads of shoppers:

some giddy, some grim, all searching for that one elusive thing
 to complete itself? I watch the bird sail through Bloomingdales

and take a balletic shit, midair, above the Le Creuset, dappling
 a Dutch oven and teakettle before it cruises into the atrium

with its oculus skylight and pitch-penny fountain, its coffee kiosk
 and neon pretzel emporium. Then it swerves up, prop plane,

into caged light and, finding no exit, down again where it perches
 on a handrail to survey a faux Eden of inedible plants, copper

colored water, and large bipeds strolling, pecking, preening in glass—
 each performing some ritual task. Habits of display, some say,

that evolve from primal shame: a reflex to hide our soft hydraulic
 parts, to disguise our bone-levers and glands as more solid, less

subject to gravity's directive. Just now, the bird alights: its wings
 wink like cufflinks past Tiffanys, a salon for the eyebrows,

a gelataria with real pistachio buttercream, before it pauses for one
 last look at this strange zoo where we conjure ourselves wild

again: without age, regret, bills, or sin. I watch a wiry mother wedge
 a jumbo stroller's regnant toddlers through double doors—

and the sparrow takes its cue: spinning the script of a triple axel into
 unclouded sky as urgently as I, without purchase, again seek you.

Acknowledgments

I am grateful to the editors of the following journals in which versions of these poems first appeared:

Bellingham Review: "Letters of Ida Bauer to Her Mother" and "Berggasse 19"

The Hopkins Review: "Sapphic"

Journal of the American Medical Association (JAMA): "Blue Madonna"

The Missouri Review: "Daphne on Being Wood," "Persephone's Postcard," and "Demeter: Calendar Girl"

Notre Dame Review: "Birth of Venus"

On the Seawall: "Quarantine"

Plume: "Tenancy," "Callas, 1954," and "Halfway"

PN Review: "Leda"

Salamander: "Cinder"

Southern Humanities Review: "Nervosa"

The Worcester Review: "Barter"

I would like to thank Anthony Walton for his steadfastness, keen eye, and relentless archive as well as Eileen Cleary for her generous support, elan, and vision. Much gratitude to my family especially my parents, Marita and Fred Treseler, and my nephews, Bjorn and Leo Treseler. Many thanks, too, to my friends and colleagues, especially Emily McMains, Rohit Chandra, and Matthew Ortoleva.

About the Author

Heather Treseler is the author of *Auguries & Divinations,* which received the 2023 May Sarton New Hampshire Poetry Prize and the 2024 Sheila Margaret Motton Book Award, and *Parturition,* which received the international chapbook prize from the Munster Literature Centre in Ireland. Her poems appear in *The American Scholar, Harvard Review, The Iowa Review, PN Review,* and *Kenyon Review,* and have received the W. B. Yeats Prize, *Narrative Magazine's* poetry prize, and the Editors' Prize at *The Missouri Review.* Her work has been supported by the National Endowment for the Humanities, the T. S. Eliot House, and the American Academy of Arts and Sciences; she is professor of English at Worcester State University and a resident scholar at the Brandeis Women's Studies Research Center.